# Secrets to Educational Success
## How YOU can be an A+ Student

## Sara Van Donge

Dedicated to my students.  I have enjoyed being your teacher.

# Secrets to Educational Success
## How YOU can be an A+ Student

# Sara Van Donge

# Secrets to Educational Success

You are a student. It is your job, whether you want it or not. You can decide if you want to be successful, but I will tell you a secret:

People who do well in school have better lives.

There. I said it. A great big generalization. But look around you. Is it true? You can argue that it isn't. I know the stories about various rock stars and executives, yes. But, for the most part, the quickest path to a pleasant life full of choices and comfort and enough free time to enjoy the things you love is…school. An education.

But, obviously, not just any education. You can't just shuffle into the easiest, lowest level class and get a low C and call it an education. That's just going through the motions. But I am here to tell you that you don't have to spend all your free time reading every page of every book and memorizing all your notes either. You can have fun, learn, enjoy your classes and get good grades. YOU can do this. Even if you have struggled in school up until this point, I will give you the tools you need to succeed.

And who am I? A public school teacher with 16 years experience. I have taught elementary school, middle school, and community college students. My main area is bilingual education. That basically means I teach people reading and writing, but in Spanish. I have been a successful teacher who helps students reach learning goals and gets good evaluations. But my main strength in life was being a good student.

A funny talent, I know. I joke about my talent now, but it really is a learned skill and not the result of some extraordinary intelligence. My standardized test scores are always right in the middle of a bell curve; I'm just average. But I know how to get really good grades and I can teach you how also. Just how good? In high school I graduated one year early and I received two B's. One B was in geometry, which I simply deserved because it was very hard for me. The other was in P.E. I was so mad!!! My friends and I ran through the sprinklers on the last day of school and I suspect the teacher might have been punishing me. Sigh, I guess I deserved that too.

In college I also earned all A's and B's while taking the maximum credit load every term. My last term I asked for permission to take extra credits so I could graduate early. I graduated with my Bachelor's degree at 19 years old. I then received a Master of Science degree (with high grades again) at the age of 20 and then completed a Master of Art in Teaching degree at the age of 21.

But I didn't just study, I was also very fun. I had a lot of friends and I went to parties often. We played sports and went camping and went to concerts and had a great time. I loved college. Even though my classes were challenging, I never crammed for a test or pulled an all-nighter or finished a paper at the last minute. In fact, I used to kick around during hell week because all my work was done. While everyone else was struggling to study and prepare for last-minute tests and papers, I wouldn't be able to find anyone to hang out with.

And remember, I wasn't anything different from anyone else in the brains department. No high IQ or gifted program for me. I was the first person in my family to go away to college and I figured out how to get through the system by playing the game right. Because it is a game, a game with rules and strategies. And I can teach you how to play, ready?

# The Tools for Success

Educational Success is the key to living the life you want to live. This book will give you the tools to succeed. After many years in the educational system, I have observed and spoken to many other successful students. We have come up with the following tools that you can use to improve your grades.

When you come to the Reading chapter you will learn to skim, to look quickly through a book to get the main ideas. You can do this now, to get the most out of this for your learning. You can flip through this book and see the chapter headings to see what the ten tools for success are. Once you are aware what successful students do, you can think about your own learning. What do you do that might hinder your learning? How can you make improvements? Make this book useful by finding the best information for you.

Before you start, think about your needs. Answer these questions:

What are your biggest difficulties in school?  Is it getting assignments or homework turned in?  Poor test scores?  Writing Essays?

What classes do you struggle with the most?  Why are you struggling?

What classes are you successful in?  Why are they easier for you?  Could you do this in other classes?

# What Do You Want?

Let's fill out some questionnaires so you know what your goals are. School is vital for your future and can be a lot of fun, but you need to make sure you are in it for the right reasons and are headed in the right direction. Make good choices when you are signing up for schools and programs and classes and you will save yourself a lot of time and effort (and probably money).

For this questionnaire write as much or as little as you want for each prompt. You can use this page or a notebook to write your answers.

Wait! Did you actually plan to write your answers? Do you have a reason why you are planning to write your answers? If you do, great! Write them down. If not, please don't write them. I wasn't actually trying to trick you, I am a teacher. Teachers can't help themselves, we just ask for students to do a lot of work. Work that may or may not be necessary for being successful in our classes or even in school. Most teachers are really invested in their own class and think what they are teaching is very important. It is important, that is why you are taking the class. But you can learn to pay attention to what needs to be done and what is just practice.

But before you invest a lot of effort and, more importantly, time, into any activity, make sure it is actually important. Look at the big picture and your overall goals and ask yourself if the activity matters. Do you really need to do the entire activity? Many times in school you can choose how much of an activity to complete to learn the necessary material. If something needs to be turned in, then absolutely turn it in. Every single time. But don't waste your time doing things that don't matter.

So back to the questionnaire. You are welcome to write down the answers. Or just read through the questionnaire and answer them in your head. But know why you are doing what you are doing. Writing down your answers will give you a more thorough understanding of yourself and your desires. Writing down your answers will also allow you to return to the book, later, in case you want to revisit these ideas.

But, really? How much time do you have? This is the number one lesson for educational success: Use Your Time Wisely. I will get to this later. But in the meantime, complete the questionnaires below in whatever way works for you.

# Your Future Goals

What are some careers you have considered?

Why do you think you would be good at these career choices?

What is your ideal future work schedule?

Do you prefer working alone, with one other person, in a small group, or with a large group?

How would you like to dress for work?

How much money do you want to earn?  Is this possible with your career choices?

How much schooling are you interested in pursuing?

What types of classes and schooling do you need to achieve your career goals?

This is intended as a guide only, something to get you thinking.  A career is not forever, but once you go to school for awhile you are pretty well invested and might need to stay with it - so choose wisely!  Take advantage of any career counseling services available at your school, read about careers you are interested in, and interview people who have your dream job.  Really research it!

# Your Educational Style

How do you keep track of your assignments, homework, essays, and test study materials?

When you are learning, do you prefer to work alone or with a partner or group?

When you do work with a partner or group, what role do you usually take?

How do you deal with a partner that is difficult to work with? Do you think you are easy to work with?

How do you prefer to get information from your teacher or professor? Do you need to see it written down or do you need to hear it?

How do you remember what you need to do for a class?

What do you do when you listen to a lecture? Do you take notes? What do your notes look like? Where do you put them afterwards? Do you look at them again?

How do you prepare for a test?  Do you prefer to study alone or with others?  Do you study one time or over a period of time?

Every person has different strengths as a learner, it is important that you think about what kind of classes work best for you.  You may not be able to control or change your classes, but in some cases you can.  If you are aware of your needs and can articulate what you need you are in a better position to communicate with your teachers and professors.

# Your Personal Life

Who are the people who matter the most to you?

What do you enjoy doing when you are with your friends?

What are your three favorite activities?

If you have a day to yourself, what do you like to do?

Are you interested in traveling?  Where would you like to go?

What other personal goals do you have for your life?

Your free time is valuable.  School and jobs are important, but so is the rest of your life.  Make sure you prioritize your interests and goals so you get to do them!

# #1 What You Do In Class

What you do in class matters.  A lot.  Teachers base their grades on many things, usually test scores.  Right now in the United States an idea called Standards Based Grading is being adopted as the best way of measuring student progress.  What does this mean?  It is supposed to mean that students are graded entirely on their performance on tests and activities related to our Common Core Standards.  Look out, though, because even as I write this there is probably somebody out there typing just as fast as I am who is trying to change those standards.  Or someone else who is arguing that schools shouldn't just grade students based on test scores, that isn't what real-life employers want.  No matter what the trend is in education, by following these simple classroom guidelines you will have the tools to be successful in school:

**1. Select a seat near the instructor so you can see and hear easily and where you are far away from people or items that might distract you**
If you are assigned a seat and it is difficult for you to see or hear or you are distracted, tell your instructor - read the chapter about talking to educators for help with this.

## 2. Arrive on time and be in your seat ready to learn before class starts

Show that you are a serious student.

## 3. Pay attention in class

This means listening, tracking, or watching the instructor and asking yourself if you understand the concepts. If you do not, ask. Every teacher has a different style, you may be able to raise your hand, ask for clarification during discussion, ask a classmate, or stay after and ask the teacher or professor. But make sure you know what you need to learn and ask for help when you need it.

## 4. Do your work in class

I know it is fun to socialize in class and it is important to be cheerful and friendly with your classmates. But most teachers give students time to complete their work in class. Use it!! Get as much homework and classwork done during class as possible, you can often talk with friends in class while you do your work. And if you work together it makes everything even easier. Don't waste your time, when you receive the assignment start working on it, get it done. Wouldn't you rather have free time after school?

## 5. Write down class information on a calendar or task list and store your materials away carefully

I will return to this in more detail in Homework and Materials. Take your time in the last minute of class. I know you are anxious to get to lunch or home or your next class, but don't be sloppy when class ends or you pay for it later. Take the extra minute to write down important information such as assignments, reading, homework, or tests before you leave. Don't waste your time writing down everything, but do write down everything you need to turn in or study. Calendars are really helpful because you can write down both when they are due and when you plan to do them. Also pack up your materials carefully, putting them in their designated spot for the class.

I want you to note that I have written the classroom guidelines in big bold lettering and I have numbered them. If you are in a hurry and only want the most important information in this book, just flip through the pages and find these lists. There are ten of them. All of the information, the writing, is just extra. This is a strategy discussed in the Reading section, a few chapters from now. So if you want some good teacher stories, continue reading. Otherwise, turn the page!

Here is an example of what an unsuccessful student does in class. I will call this first guy Chip because I have never had a Chip in my class, so if you were one of my students and for some reason you are reading this - I am not talking about you!

Meet Chip:  The guy who doesn't know what to do with
his time in class

Chip slides into class either just as the bell rings or even afterward.  As class begins, he is wandering around, looking for materials, and looking at other students.  He sits in his seat, but doesn't bother to turn to face the teacher, he is instead facing one of his friends.  The teacher has to ask him to turn around.  The class begins a discussion, but Chip is not able to participate, he has no idea what is happening or what they are talking about.  When the instructor hands out the assignment, he explains it will be homework if it is not completed in class.  Chip starts telling his friend about a recent game he played and doesn't begin the assignment.  When the bell rings to dismiss the class, Chip stuffs his blank assignment into his already stuffed-full backpack.  That night when his parents ask why he has an F, Chip blames the teacher, saying the class is too boring or too hard.

# #2 Your Materials

You need materials as a student and it is your job to make sure you are prepared with the right materials every day. You don't need anything fancy or expensive but if you don't have the basics life can get stressful quickly. Keeping your materials organized will make your life much easier. Follow these quick tips for education success:

## 1. Begin class with all materials prepared

I know I already wrote this in the previous chapter, but it is worth mentioning twice. Be prepared at the beginning of class. When you sit down, pull out everything you will need to make sure you are ready.

## 2. Keep each class separate

Everyone needs their own system. Some people like a binder with sections. Some people like individual notebooks. Some people like folders. I know a lot of instruction is done on the computer and a lot of people like to take notes on laptops, but I encourage you to also have a system for keeping track of your physical materials.

## 3. A Calendar or Task List

Write it down and it will happen. A task list is where you write down what you need to do and check it off as it is done; this gives a lot of people a sense of accomplishment. Calendars are great because they let you write down deadlines for school assignments and tests as well as personal activities. Calendars are also really useful because you can write down when you will do your work, not just when it is due. This can be on a paper calendar or a virtual laptop, tablet, or smart phone. Whatever system you use make sure you are consistent. Though it can be hard to see the big picture on a virtual calendar, calendars on smart phones and laptops are very convenient.

## Meet Cheery: The Girl who doesn't organize her materials.

Cheery arrives on time to class, but sits talking with a friend until the bell rings. She doesn't open her backpack or prepare any materials. A few minutes into class his instructor asks everyone to begin writing but Cheery realizes she doesn't have a pencil. She asks her classmates for pencils but they are all busy, they want to complete their work so they don't have homework that night. She gets out of her seat to ask her teacher for a pencil. The teacher is surprised it took this long to ask, but gives Cheery a pencil so she can begin working. Just as Cheery gets her name on her paper and starts to read the first sentence, her classmates begin to finish their work. She doesn't look as she shoves it into her full backpack and it gets very wrinkly, she figures she will straighten it out later when she does it that night. Before the bell rings the teacher tells everyone they have a test the next day and tells them to write down the chapter they should read so they can study. Cheery finds a scrap of paper and writes the information, she will find this scrap of paper later too. When she leaves she drops the pencil, but doesn't bother to pick it up. That night when it is time to do her homework, Cheery can't remember what class the piece of paper was for. She throws it away. She tries to finish the assignment, but it has gotten so wrinkly and ripped after being in her backpack all day that she has trouble reading it. Cheery shrugs and decides it probably isn't that important anyway.

# #3 Taking Notes

Professors and teachers lecture.  As students go further in education and take more advanced classes, they need to learn how to take notes that are useful.  Taking notes is an important way to listen, learn, and be able to review information from class.  But good note-taking skills are not something that we are just born knowing and they don't need to be complicated.  Follow these steps to note-taking success:

**1.  Always label your notes with a consistent heading before you begin taking notes**
Some schools will tell you how to label your notes, if they do you are lucky, follow their guidelines.  If not, come up with something you like that includes your name, the date, and the class period at the top of the page.

**2.  Give your notes a title**
You may not know the title at the beginning of the lecture, but eventually you need to understand the MAIN IDEA of the lecture.  Make this main idea the title of the notes.

### 3. Leave a space to the side for writing important information

This can be as small as the margin or as big as 1/3 of the paper, it depends on your preference. But make sure you have a place to write down extra information, important information, or vocabulary. Do you have a question you want to ask the teacher or lecturer after the lecture? Write it here. Is something probably going to be on the test? Then write the word TEST and draw a little arrow. These are your notes, make them useful for yourself.

### 4. Only write down the important information

This means key words, vocabulary, big ideas, dates. Remember, the lecture is a time to listen. Follow what the speaker is saying and write things down quickly as you hear them. If you have trouble doing both at the same time, listen first and write down just a few key words to help you remember. Even writing down parts of words or very quick sketches will help jar your memory if you are paying attention and listening to the lecture.

### 5. Make really important information jump out at you

Underline, circle, highlight. Develop your own system. I like to circle the word that shows biggest idea and underline the words that explain this idea. Why? When I read it again that night it takes about 45 seconds because I'm skimming over all those extra words and just seeing the important words. If you really want to make it fun, take notes with some colored pens, blocking stuff into different segments. It keeps you interested in the lecture too.

## 6. Review your notes often

It is important that you review your notes often. Don't wait until the night before the test. Take just a couple of minutes every day to look over all of your notes from your classes. This is how you will get the information into your long-term memory. If you review daily you won't have to spend much time studying right before tests, you will know the information, and isn't this the real goal?


Meet Scat: The guy who doesn't take useful notes


Scat's teacher was giving a lecture to the class. The information would be on the upcoming test. Scat had a piece of paper but it had some other writing on it. Scat didn't have time to write his name, the date, or the class information, because he was trying to write down everything the teacher said. Scat quickly got lost because the teacher was talking too fast. Scat eventually started copying the girl next to him, but she was so far ahead he wasn't really listening to the teacher at all. By the time the lecture was over Scat wasn't sure what the teacher had been talking about. That night he pulled the notes out so he could study for the test, but he had trouble finding which of his pages of notes belonged to which class. He didn't understand what most of the notes meant and hadn't labeled any of the pages. He didn't really review the information and didn't do very well on the test.

# #4 Reading

You will need to read to learn new information in every class you take.  The more advanced the class, the more reading you will need to do on your own.  But you won't always have time to read every single word that you are expected to read.  In fact this would not be a good use of your time.  Reading informational texts to learn is very different, and in many ways, easier, than reading a novel for fun.  Check out these tips, do them, and see if your assignment is completed more quickly, with less effort, and with better understanding.

You are not reading for fun.  You are reading to learn.  Your time is precious.  Do not waste your time reading things you already know, things that are unrelated to your coursework, or things that won't be on your test.  Cynical, I know, but your time is precious.  If you love the text book and want to read it for fun, then read it for fun.  But if you have to read it for a class, use these methods to make it worth your effort.

### 1. Always do the reading

When an educator asks you to read, be that star student who actually opens the book. But… keep reading for ways to make your time count.

## 2.  Skim

Use your pointer finger and move it over the page, quickly.  You are looking for things that jump out at you.  Text that is different, captions below pictures, headings at the beginning of paragraphs, bold vocabulary and definitions.  Read the chapter titles, introduction, and conclusion.  Get an idea what this book is about before you read anything.

## 3.  Be an Active Reader

Have a pencil in your hand, jot down notes about the most important information which usually includes key words, chapter and section headings, and summaries.  If you can write in the book, underline, circle, or highlight key ideas and words and write clarifications in the margins.  Use sticky notes to mark interesting or important information.  Your goal is to identify the MAIN IDEAS and help yourself remember them later.

## 4.  Take notes as you read

This is done exactly the same way as if you were listening to a lecture.  Write your heading, leave a space for questions and main ideas and vocabulary, and write the most important information down.

## 5.  Be prepared with things to say about the reading

Arrive in class the next day prepared to speak about what you have read. This is for two reasons. First, it will demonstrate to your teacher that you care about your learning. Second, it will make classwork and discussion mean something. You will know what is going on in class.

How do you do this? By bringing your notes to class, having them ready on your desk when class begins. And by finding one thing that really interests you to talk about. Write it on your notes so you remember.

## Meet Spacey: The girl who wastes her time with reading

Spacey hates reading assignments. When the teacher tells the class to read 40 pages of the science book, Spacey lugs her book home and does exactly what she is supposed to. It is so boring, it takes forever and she can never even remember what she read. The worst part is, Spacey's best friend, Cheery, does the reading in about ten minutes and remembers everything. Cheery can talk at the length about the reading the next day. All Cheery does is flip through the book, highlight a couple of things, jot down a few words, and then she wastes the rest of the time texting her boyfriend. It really bugs Spacey, especially because Spacey highlights the entire book as she reads it and still can't tell anyone what she just read. Spacey wishes she didn't have to read anything for another class again!

# #5 Writing Essays

Writing essays is a big part of education, especially the further you go in school. I will cover some basic ideas for getting essays completed here. For more information on how to write essay, read, 'Secrets to Essay Writing Success', where you can learn methods for pain-free essay writing. For the basics on looking at the big picture of essay writing, read on…

**1. Make a plan**

Please know what you are writing about before you begin writing. It does not matter what type of organization you use, it can be a list or or an outline (my favorite) or a summary. Just know what you are writing about. A really well organized essay is planned out before you write it, so the writing should not be painful and if you are doing research you know what you are looking for.

**2. Introduction. Body. Conclusion.**

The most basic essay has an introduction (I am a going to write about _____), a body (Let me tell you five things about _____), and a conclusion (Now you know about _____). But even really advanced essays have an introduction, body, and conclusion. Make sure yours essay does too.

### 3. Just write

Once you have a plan and, if necessary, some quotes or information from books, write. The best writing, even technical writing, sounds like you are speaking. Don't correct yourself or wonder if it sounds silly or if it's going to get a good grade. Just get it on the paper as fast as humanly possible. If you can't type, dictate it into a phone or computer or have someone else type it for you.

### 4. Read your writing!

I put an exclamation point on this one because if you do #3 and then don't do #4 it is possible that you will turn in an absolutely terrible paper that makes no sense. Or maybe a comical paper that your teacher will bring to the staff lounge to share with his friends. This would happen if you were trying to write a formal essay but used informal language, for example. Know your audience! Read your paper, aloud, and fix it. You can write over the top of any errors or strange or overly-informal sounding language and make your paper turn-in-ready.

### 5. Make a final draft

Take the time to rewrite or type out a final draft of your paper. Neatness counts and it counts a lot. If an educator can't read your work, it is really hard to give a good score. And hey, if you don't care enough about your grades to take the time to do it right - why should your teacher care enough to take her time to try to decipher it?  Sloppy papers get low grades.


## Meet Poky: The guy who gets really stressed out about writing a paper

Poky's school year is not going well.  He has two different teachers that love assigning essays to the class. Poky hates writing papers!  He just can't get started and never knows what to write down.  He puts it off until the day before the paper is due and then sits up all night at the computer, sweating and unable to write.  He watches his friend Chip make a quick outline as the teacher describes the assignment.  Then Chip seems to be able to write his essay without any stress at all.  Chip never has to miss any parties while Poky slaves away for hours at the computer, Poky just wishes he could get these papers over with.

# #6 Working in Groups

Working with a partner or in groups is becoming increasingly more common for graded work. Your ability to work with others can effect your learning and even your grade. Make the most of working with other people. It can be fun and, in many cases, you can get more done and learn more when you have hep from your classmates. You may find that working with classmates is useful for you as a learner and you may choose to form study groups of your own later.

### 1. Choose people who you work with productively

If you have the option, choose classmates who are a good learning match for you. Successful students don't always choose to work with their best friends, although your friends may be a good choice if they are also enthusiastic learners.

### 2. Be a positive and productive part of the group

Working with a group is not always easy, but your attitude can make all the difference. Do your group a favor: stay upbeat and be agreeable.

### 3. Listen to your teammates

Every person in the group is valuable, show kindness to people in your group by listening to them as they share their ideas.

### 4. Participate and encourage others to participate

Everyone needs to be a part of the group. For some people this is easy, for others they hold back. Step forward and lead if necessary but don't always be the only one who does anything, it is important that every person have a chance to contribute. Oh the other hand, if you are reluctant to participate, remember that you will benefit more from the experience if you put forth effort and give your 100%.

### 5. Complete your share of the work and encourage others to complete theirs

It is your responsibility to do your work, make sure you get it done as soon as you can. If you have a group member or partner who is not pulling their weight, speak directly to them about it. Part of the work of group work is collaborating and negotiating with other people, if you are direct and respectful your task will be easier.

Jolly, Spacey, and Chip: The students who do not work well as a team

Whenever Jolly has to work with a group, his classmates are not eager to work with him. He is fun, but he will not stay on task and is constantly distracting his team members.  Jolly is so busy making jokes and playing he keeps his team from getting almost anything done. Spacey tries to keep the group on task, but when it comes time to discuss the subject matter she dominates the conversation and argues about everyone else's suggestions. Chip would prefer to work alone, he could accomplish the task much more quickly without having to deal with other people.  He spends most of the group time sitting in silence, working alone and ignoring his team.  When it is time to turn in the project Spacey turns it in on her own, mad at the rest of the team for not doing their share.  Their grade is lowered because they did not all participate.

# #7 Talking to Educators

Speaking to your instructors is one of the most important secrets of educational success. Educators have many students and they want them to succeed. If they know a student is serious about being successful, a teacher will almost always help wherever possible.

## 1. Have a plan before you approach your teacher

Be specific when you talk to an instructor about your grade. Do not ask how you can get your grade up, that is too broad and shows you are passive about your education. If you pay attention and turn in what you are supposed to, you will know exactly why you have a lower grade than you desire. Ask specifically if you can redo or add to an assignment you did not do well on or retake a test. Your grade is not arbitrary, it is based on your scores. Many times scores can be improved it you ask.

## 2. Speak to your instructor at a good time

Pay attention to your teacher and wait until he or she is not busy before you speak about your grade. The best times are after class hours or during planning or office hours. If possible, find a moment during class when your teacher is not teaching, when all of the students are occupied, and ask if there is a good time to speak to him or her. Emailing your teacher with specific questions can be helpful also.

### 3. Take care of your tests and assignments quickly!

Do not approach your teacher at the end of the term and ask to redo tests or assignments or to turn in late assignments. This just shows that you are irresponsible. Take care of low grades as soon as they happen, speak to your teacher within three days of receiving your test or or assignment score.

Poky: The guy who doesn't know how to speak to his instructors

Poky is getting a D in one of his classes. He was not worried about his grades when he received low grades on his tests and now he thinks it is possible he didn't turn in some assignments, though he isn't sure. The end of the term is only a few days away, so he knows he needs to do something about his grade. At the beginning of class, as the teacher is calling the students to attention, Poky approaches him. Poky asks what he needs to do to make his grade an A. The teacher asks Poky to sit down and to return after class . When Poky comes in after class, the teacher gives him a long list of assignments that have not been turned in. Poky is annoyed about the amount of work he has to do. He does a sloppy job on a few assignments and turns them in. Poky ends up with a low C in the class.

# #8 Study Skills

When studying, think of the tortoise and the hare: slow and steady wins the race. Your goal with education is to learn, right? Yes, you want to be successful and get good grades, but you want to actually know the material. This is the true goal and the best way to do very well in class. Knowing the subject matter, thoroughly understanding it, is the best secret to educational success. And this is not about being intelligent as much as it is about being intelligent about how you learn.

### 1. Your Study Spot

Make sure you have a designated place to study. Well lit, free of distraction, and comfortable. It is important that you have a place to study and complete assignments and homework that is conducive to learning.

### 2. Time

Make it a habit to study nightly.

Don't lose the learning and information you have gained, review your notes every night. It isn't necessary to look at them for long, just long enough to allow your brain to slide that new knowledge into your long-term memory.

### 3. Know your learning style

Be aware of how you learn best and take advantage of this knowledge as you help yourself master your subject matter. Do you learn best while reading? Will making up a song or a movement set to the information help you remember? Does working with other people help you learn better? Find your strengths and use them to your own learning advantage.

Spacey: The girl who does not study effectively

Spacey is struggling to do well in her classes, especially with her test scores. She crams for hours the night before the test only to wake up the next morning unable to remember any of the information. Seeing her friend Cheery hardly study at all - just a couple of minutes a night - and then get an A - is frustrating. Spacey really wants to do well but just can't seem to remember the information. Scat and Chip don't seem to have any trouble remembering things either, but they sing these silly songs listing the facts and Spacey is just too embarrassed to join in. She just wishes she knew how to study better.

# #9 Test Taking

Taking tests in a big part of being in school. In some cases your test scores will be the only measurement used to give you your class grade and I'm sure you already know how important your tests are. Students who get high test scores generally WANT really high test scores. They do everything they can to ensure they do as well as possible on tests. First off, you will need to know what will be on the test and study it. This seems obvious, right? It is amazing how many students do not notice when their educators tell them outright that information will be on the test. Your teachers want you to do well, they want to give you access to the information you will need for assessments. Pay attention, ask what is on the test, and study this information for a few minutes every day. But today's student is not just tested on memorized facts or new ideas. Our national standards are moving more and more to an assessment of analytical thinking skills. How well can you read information and interpret meaning? State tests are not testing what you know. State tests are testing what you can do with information already presented to you.

For this reason, it is important that you learn some of the best strategies used by successful students.

### 1. Read the directions carefully

Pay attention to what you really need to be doing with test questions. Many tests consist of reading a lot of information and looking for examples within the text to demonstrate what you know. In many cases there will be two steps to the question or more than one example. Read the directions carefully and be aware of your task before you begin.

### 2. Read the problems or questions before you begin reading large quantities of text

Right along with being aware of directions before you begin, flip past any reading and look at the questions. In some cases this can save you time, you may find the answers or examples before you finish reading. Knowing what you are looking for also gives you an understanding of what is most important with the text or information.

### 3. Read every answer option

Even if you think the first answer is correct, read every option because there may be one of those tricky All Of The Above answers.

### 4. If possible, skip difficult questions and come back to them later

Complete problems and questions that are easy for you as quickly as possible, while your brain is fresh and you are feeling energized. The possibility of getting these right is much higher than questions you do not know, so your best bet is to complete all of these, especially if the test is timed. If this is a standardized test where you are filling in bubbles, however, do not skip difficult questions. The risk of getting mixed up with the bubbles is too high. Instead, if you are doing a bubble fill-in test and don't know the answer, guess the best answer as quickly as you can and move on. Your goal in doing this is to avoid getting stressed out about the test.

### 5. Making an educated guess

There will be times when you have to guess, so be smart about it. Eliminate any obviously wrong answers and choose from the remaining possibilities.

### 6. Go back and check your answers

Teachers always tell you to do this, but what does that mean? It means you go through the test and look at every single question and answer them again, in your head. Did you pick the same answer this time? Can you locate the answer in the reading or problem? Did you redo any math problems to make sure your work is done carefully? Take this time to check.

### 7. If you are feeling tired or stressed out, get up and get a drink

Most teachers will let you get up during a test unless you are notoriously rude or disruptive. If you start feeling lost or disinterested, get out of your seat. Get blood flowing to your head, take deep breaths and drink water. This will help you think when you return to your test.

## 8. Be healthy

Teachers are always telling kids to get a good night's sleep and eat breakfast before they take a test. Do you know why? Because this will help you achieve. If you stay up late studying or eat or drink something sweet before the test, your energy will be low and your brain won't be functioning as well as it should. Go to bed early and eat a high-protein breakfast for test-taking success.

Jolly: The guy who doesn't do very well on tests

Jolly gets really nervous for tests. He tries to study right up to the minute the test starts, but he still ends up getting really stressed out. He always reads any long passages completely, but when it's time to answer questions or look for information, he can't even remember what he read about. Then Jolly gets bogged down on one or two problems, sometimes spending most of the test time on just a couple of things. He can hardly ever even finish the test. He is tired of failing tests.

# #10 Homework

Doing homework is an inevitable part of being a student, but spending hours every night is not. When you decide to be a successful student, you need a plan for completing your homework and getting it turned in every day.

### 1. Organization

As a successful student, you should already be storing your papers in a designated space for each class as well as writing down your homework assignments. This is key for getting your homework completed, as is returning your completed homework to it's class section and making sure your backpack or bag is ready to go so you never scramble to find things in the morning.

### 2. Space and Distraction

As with studying, make sure you have a good place to study and no distractions. You want to get your homework done quickly, right? Then sit down in a quiet place and get it done. Don't have the TV or music on, it makes your homework take much longer.

### 3. Can you do it at school?

It is amazing how long it takes for some students just to take a homework page or write down a homework assignment. Most successful students will at least begin their homework assignment as the less serious students joke around and waste time. Teachers like to take time to explain homework, maybe to tell you when it is due or how important it is. If you can do so without being rude or disrespectful, try to begin your homework when it is handed out. An added bonus to this is it allows you to notice any questions you might have about the assignment so you can ask after class if necessary. Just make sure you aren't so busy doing the homework you miss the explanation and then have to go ask for the teacher to re-explain! Pay attention.

Chip: The guy who doesn't get his homework done

Chip was struggling to turn in his homework. When his teachers passed out homework assignments Chip would usually take that time to talk and joke with his friends in class. He often ended up shoving the homework into his backpack without looking at it or putting it in the right class section. When he got home from school, he did not have a set time when he did homework, but if he thought of it and tried to find any assignments he would get confused about which paper went with which class. Just finding the right papers to do took a long time and by the time Chip sat down in front of the TV to try to finish he had a really hard time concentrating. Chip's teachers were really starting to bug him about getting his homework assignments in and it seemed like every year he had more homework than the year before. He needed help!

# Your Success Depends on You

School is what you make of it!  By following these ten secrets to educational success you can reach your goals and enjoy a successful and pleasant life.

You may think you can't do this.  You may think you aren't smart enough, but intelligence has nothing to do with how well you do in school.  Yes, your intelligence may effect how many times you have to look at something before you remember it.  Your intelligence may effect how many different ways you need to learn about something before it makes sense to you or how often you need to review things to not forget them.  But school success is not about intelligence.  School success is about following the right rules and doing the right activities.  School success is about being able to see the big picture and following directions.

You may also think being a successful student requires a lot of time.  I can absolutely tell you that this is not true!  The opposite in fact, if you use your time wisely from the very beginning of the class term, you will have more free time.  You will have more time to be with the people you care about and to do the activities that you love if you are organized and manage your time, materials, and choices of activities. Again, school success is about seeing everything as a whole and deciding what is the most important. You can do this, anyone can if they choose to and know the rules.

# Visualization

Now it is time to see yourself as a successful student. Studies show that people who are confident and can visualize their success have a much higher chance of actually meeting their goals. Practice visualization throughout your day, not just for school success but to achieve personal goals too. It doesn't take long. Even just a few seconds with your eyes closed, seeing yourself succeed, can give you the confidence to actually go out there and do it. There are as many different ways of practicing visualization as there people, so find a way that works for you. Here is one example:

Either read this and then try it or have a friend read it to you while you sit comfortably with your eyes closed.

1. You are in your most difficult class. See yourself in detail. Where are you seated? Have you selected a seat near the instructor where you can see and hear easily? Are you far away from people or items that might distract you?

2. Look at your materials. Imagine they are all organized and you have everything you need for the class before class begins.

3. See your calendar or task list. Imagine you have checked off all necessary tasks for this class and are prepared before class begins. Do you have a piece of paper and a pencil in front of you? Do you need any other materials for this class?

4. As the class begins, see yourself listening, tracking the instructor and understanding the concepts. You are nodding and actively listening.

5. See yourself taking notes. How are you organizing your notes? Are you writing down just the most important information, highlighting the key words and important vocabulary?

6. If this class has any individual reading, see yourself as an active reader. Is there a pencil in your hand? Are you jotting down notes about the most important information? Are you skimming to find out what the most important parts of the reading are? Are you looking for key words, chapter and section headings, and summaries? If you can, are you underlining key ideas and words? See yourself doing this quickly and easily, grasping the MAIN IDEAS of what you are reading.

7. If this class requires you to work with others, see yourself being a productive and positive partner. Are you listening to others by looking at them, asking questions, and taking turns? Do you volunteer to participate? Do you

let others participate? Do you complete the work and help your group stay on task? See yourself having fun with your group or partner, working with other students is fun, imagine yourself smiling and getting the work done quickly and easily.

8. See yourself talking to your instructor. Did you wait until after class when the instructor was not busy? Did you ask if it was a good time? See the conversation going well, both of you are professional and interested in seeing you get an A. Imagine yourself as an equal partner with your teacher or professor, you are both interested in you being successful in this class.

9. See yourself packing up your materials. Are you carefully putting them in their designated spot for the class? Did you write down any homework or studying you will do and when you will do it? See yourself slowly and carefully storing all your papers and materials where they belong.

10. Finally, see yourself at home, in your designated study spot. You are studying or completing work for this class. You aren't working for very long, you are energized and entirely focused on this work, you know it will be completed very quickly and successfully. See yourself with a smile, this is easy for you and you know your work at home will make you very successful the next day and for the rest of the term. Then see yourself putting all your materials away and placing them where they need to be for the next school day.

# YOU ARE A SUCCESSFUL STUDENT

# Goal Setting

This is your time to take action and be a successful student! You are capable and you now have the skills to achieve. Make an academic goal for yourself and stick to it. Use this template to complete a goal for yourself.

Educational Goal:

By _____ (date) I will improve by _____ (specific grade or percentage) in _____ (class).
I will improve by _____ (specific activities).

You can also set goals for your future career and for personal dreams. Just make sure you have a date to reach the goal and that you list specific activities that you will do to meet the goal. Goal-setting is key to living the life you want. Think back to the questionnaires you completed at the beginning of this book. What goals can you set related to your career? Try setting short-term and long-term goals related to your career. Write them down, you may surprise yourself years from now when you see that you have done exactly what you wanted.

Personal goals are also very important and can be fun to think about and write down. Think about traveling and friendships and relationships. What do you want to do?

Where do you want to live? What type of house and car do you want? The world can be open to you if you make decisions and have a good education.

Chip, Cheery, and Jolly: The kids who like setting goals.

Chip successfully reached this educational goal:
By the end of first quarter I will improve by 20%, from a C to an A, in Math. I will improve by arriving on time to class, writing down homework assignments turning, and studying every night from 5:00 - 5:30.

Cheery successfully reached this educational goal:
By the end of the term I will raise my grade from an 80% to at least a 90% in Science. I will do this by being prepared for class and reading using strategies to find the main idea.

And Jolly successfully reached this educational goal:
By the end of this school year I will improve my state tests by 20 points in both reading and math. I will do this by getting a good night's sleep the night before. I will also read the directions and the questions before reading any passages and make educated guesses if I'm not sure about the answer.

How about you? What kind of goals are you going to set? You too can make goals and meet them. It is time to be a successful student and enjoy your life!

S Van Donge

Sara Van Donge is a 16-year veteran public school teacher. She has taught every grade level from Kindergarten through 8th Grade as well as Community College language classes. Sara is a Spanish speaking bilingual teacher who helped start a dual language program in Walla Walla. She has a Bachelor of Science degree from Eastern Oregon University in Bilingual and Hispanic Studies. She also has a Master of Science degree in Information and Technology as well as Bilingual Studies from Western Oregon University. She certified to teach through the Master of Arts in Teaching program at Eastern Oregon University.

In her free time, Sara enjoys spending time with her family in Walla Walla. She loves biking, reading, and cooking. Sara is also the author of 'I Love Love Walla Walla', 'Dutch Jo's Good Time Girls', and 'Rock on Sister.' Her next Secrets to Educational Success book, 'Essay Writing', will be out in Spring of 2015. For more information on her latest projects and to sign up for her mailing list, go to her website at platformpublishers.com.

S Van Donge